TELL ME MORE! science

FUNGI

Colorful Clean-Up Crews

by Ruth Owen

Ruby Tuesday Books

Published in 2021 by Ruby Tuesday Books Ltd.

Consultant: Ali McKernan – The FUNgi Guy
Designer: Emma Randall
Editor: Mark J. Sachner
Production: John Lingham

Photo credits:
Nature Picture Library: Cover, 12, 13; Shutterstock: 1, 4, 5, 6–7, 8, 9, 10–11, 14, 15, 16, 17, 18, 19, 20, 21, 22, 23.

Library of Congress Control Number: 2020946812
Print (hardback) ISBN 978-1-78856-159-4
Print (paperback) ISBN 978-1-78856-160-0
eBook ISBN 978-1-78856-161-7

Printed and published in the United States of America
For further information including rights and permissions requests,
please contact: **shan@rubytuesdaybooks.com**

Contents

Many types of fungi are poisonous. Never touch a fungus you see growing in a forest, field, or any other outdoor place.

DANGER

DANGER

What Is a Fungus?

A fungus is a living thing that can grow and **reproduce**. It can even find food for itself.

Is a fungus a type of plant or an animal? No!

Fungi are living things in a group of their own that scientists call the **fungal kingdom**.

Bleeding tooth fungus

This fungus is called a bleeding tooth fungus because it oozes a red liquid.

This fungus helps clean up dead tree trunks and branches by feeding on them.

Its nickname is the turkey tail fungus.

Turkey tail fungus

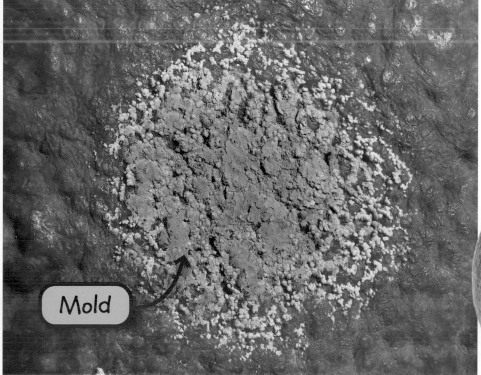

Mold

The **mold** that grows on old bread or fruit is also a type of fungus.

The Parts of a Fungus

Most of the time we can't see a fungus. Why?

A fungus is made of very thin threads called **hyphae** (HI-fee).

The hyphae often grow underground in soil or inside rotting logs and branches.

Together, the hyphae make a **mycelium** (my-SEAL-e-um).

When it is time to reproduce, the mycelium produces a **fruiting body** that we can see.

Inside a piece of rotting wood.

Fruiting body

Cap

Hyphae

Stem, or stipe

Mycelium

Fruiting bodies come in many different shapes. A fruiting body with a cap and a stalk is called a mushroom or toadstool.

Making More Fungi

Inside a fruiting body there are millions of **spores**.

Each **microscopic** spore contains everything that's needed to grow a new fungus.

Fungi spores spread to new growing places in lots of ways.

A puffball fungus puffs a cloud of spores into the air to be spread by the wind.

Millions of spores

Puffball fungus

The spores of an octopus stinkhorn fungus are on its finger-like fruiting body.

The sticky fingers smell like rotting meat, which attracts flies.

Fruiting body

Octopus stinkhorn fungus

Let's Talk
The flies help spread the octopus stinkhorn's spores. How?

(The answer is on page 24.)

Fungi Clean-Up Crews

Many kinds of fungi live and feed on dead wood.

Their hyphae spread through the wood, taking in **nutrients**.

The hyphae also take in water.

As the hyphae spread, they help break down the dead wood and make it rot faster.

Some fungi feed on old leaves or the bodies of dead animals. Without this helpful clean-up crew there would be lots of rotting stuff lying around!

This jelly-like black fungus feeds on dead wood. It got its name because it is soft and greasy.

Fantastic Fungi

The eyelash fungus lives and feeds on rotting wood.

It has cup-shaped fruiting bodies with eyelash-like hairs.

Eyelash fungus

This fungus is so tiny that a row of five cups might only measure 1 inch (2.5 cm) long.

These glowing mushrooms are feeding on dead twigs, branches, and logs.

In the day, they look brownish-gray. But at night, they glow green.

Glowing mushrooms

The green light is made by chemicals inside the mushrooms. Scientists have studied this fungus, but no one has figured out why it glows green—yet!

Parasitic Fungi

Some fungi live and feed on trees and other plants that are still alive.

Honey fungus and chicken of the woods live in this way.

These fungi are **parasitic**.

Parasitic fungi harm and even kill the plants they live on.

Honey fungus

It might seem like a bad thing when a parasitic fungus kills a tree. But the dead tree will become food for insects and fungi that feed on rotting wood.

Chicken of the woods

Let's Talk
How do you think chicken of the woods got its name?

(The answer is on page 24.)

Helpful Fungi

Some fungi, such as shaggy ink caps and giant puffballs, grow around the roots of plants and work with them as a team. How?

Shaggy ink cap fungus

The cap of a shaggy ink cap oozes a black liquid that contains its spores. The liquid looks like dripping black ink.

The fungus's hyphae spread out and collect water and nutrients from the soil.

The plant's roots share the water and nutrients in the hyphae.

Giant puffball fungus

The plant makes sugary food that it stores in its roots.

The hyphae share some of the high-energy food made by the plant.

Poisonous Fly Agarics

The spotty fly **agaric** is a very poisonous type of fungus.

It lives by sharing water and nutrients with trees in return for sugary food.

Fly agaric mushroom

In **Victorian** times, these mushrooms were used to kill flies. People put pieces of smelly fly agaric in a dish of milk to attract the insects. When the flies landed on the dish, they were poisoned!

As this mushroom grows, it is protected by a white covering.

The covering splits as the young mushroom's cap gets bigger.

Young fly agaric

White covering

The fly agaric's white spots are tiny pieces of its covering that are stuck to its red cap.

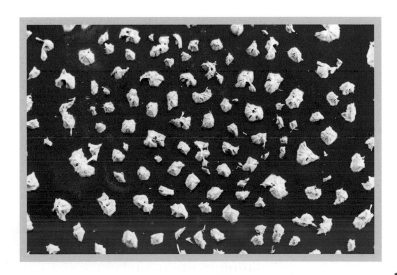

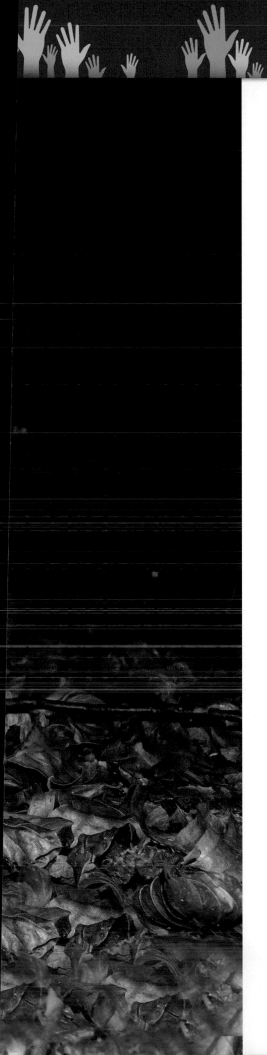

Mushroom Farms

The mushrooms we buy from grocery stores are fungi that grow on farms.

To grow mushrooms, spores are mixed into **compost** made from horse **manure** and straw.

Mushrooms are a type of fruiting body.

Let's Talk

How are fungi similar to and different from plants?

(There are some ideas on page 24.)

20

The compost is laid out in mushroom beds in warm, dark rooms called cells.

The spores grow into new fungi with fruiting bodies that can be picked for eating.

Mushroom *bed*

Compost

Many fungi grow fruiting bodies in autumn, when it's cool. To make the fungi on a farm start producing mushrooms, the temperature in the cells is lowered.

Be a Mushroom Scientist

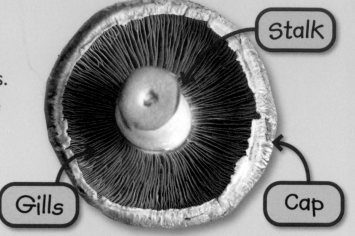

Stalk

Gills

Cap

You should never touch mushrooms or other fungi that you see growing outdoors because some are poisonous. But it's safe to investigate the fungi we can buy in food stores.

If you look under a mushroom's cap, you can see parts called gills.

The spores are inside the gills.

It's possible to see the microscopic spores by making a spore print.

Gather Your Equipment:

- Large, fresh mushrooms with gills
- A small table knife
- White paper
- A small glass bowl
- A magnifying glass

1. It's important that your mushrooms are fresh and have not been in a refrigerator. Before starting, store your mushroom right way up, in a cool, dry place for two days.

2. Ask an adult to help you cut the stalk from the mushroom. Also, carefully trim the edge of the mushroom cap so the gills will lie flat against the paper.

3. Place the mushroom on the paper with the gills facing down.

4. Cover the mushroom with a small glass bowl. This will help keep the air damp around the mushroom so it releases spores. It also keeps the tiny spores from being disturbed.

5. Leave the mushroom and bowl in place for 24 hours.

6. Carefully remove the bowl and very gently lift up the mushroom.

7. Finally, examine your spore print with a magnifying glass.

Glossary

agaric
The science word for a fungus fruiting body with a cap and stalk.

compost
Soil that is used for growing plants and mushrooms. Compost is made from materials such as dead leaves or animal manure.

fruiting body
The part of a fungus that contains spores for reproduction. A fruiting body with a cap and stalk is known as a mushroom or toadstool.

fungal kingdom
The group name for all the different types of fungi. Scientists think there are about 1.5 million different kinds.

hyphae
Thin threads that grow from a fungus spore. The hyphae take in water and nutrients for the fungus. A single thread is called a hypha (HI-fa).

manure
Another word for animal waste, or poop.

microscopic
So tiny it can only be seen through a microscope.

mold
A type of soft, crumbly fungus that grows and feeds on materials such as old food or dead leaves.

mycelium
The part of a fungus made up of many hyphae. The fruiting bodies grow from the mycelium.

nutrients
Substances that are needed by living things to help them grow and stay healthy.

parasitic
Living in or on another living thing and feeding off it. A parasitic fungus, plant, or animal often harms the thing it lives on.

reproduce
To make more of something.

spore
A tiny part of a fungus that contains everything needed to grow a new fungus. Spores act a little like a plant's seeds.

Victorian
A time in history from about 150 years ago. It is named after Queen Victoria, who was a British queen.

Stags horn fungus

Index

Read More

Owen, Ruth. *Welcome to the Forest (Nature's Neighborhoods: All About Ecosystems)*. Minneapolis, MN: Ruby Tuesday Books (2016).

Owen, Ruth. *What's the Season? (Get Started With STEM)*. Minneapolis, MN: Ruby Tuesday Books (2017).

Answers

Page 9:
Flies land on the octopus stinkhorn's fruiting body because it smells like rotting meat. Flies lay their eggs on rotting meat so their larvae, or young, have something to eat when they hatch. As the flies investigate the octopus stinkhorn fungus, spores stick to them. Then, when the insects fly away, they carry some spores with them to new growing places.

Page 15:
Some fungus experts pick chicken of the woods fungus and cook it. They say it tastes and feels like chicken, which is how it got its nickname. You should never touch a fungus you see outdoors, though. Only experts should do this. Some animals, including beetles and deer, eat chicken of the woods.

Page 20:
Some fungi grow in soil, just like plants. Fungi have hyphae to take in water and nutrients, while plants use their roots to do this. Both fungi and plants can reproduce. Fungi produce fruiting bodies filled with spores. Most plants grow their seeds in flowers and fruits. Spores and some seeds are tiny, but each one can grow into a new living thing. Some plants and fungi are food for animals and people.